2-

Return to Steam

Return to Steam

Steam Tours on British Rail from 1969

David Eatwell and John H Cooper-Smith

FITZHOUSE BOOKS
LONDON

© David Eatwell and John H Cooper-Smith 1978
First published 1978
Reprinted 1983

ISBN 0 7134 0864 2

Printed and bound in Great Britain by
Anchor Brendon Ltd, Tiptree, Essex
for the Publishers B T Batsford Limited
4 Fitzhardinge Street London W1H 0AH

Contents

Introduction

This pictorial survey of steam on British Rail since 'The 1968 Ban' displays as varied and interesting a selection of photographs as possible. About fifty locomotives are shown, in places as far apart as the West Country and Scotland, East Anglia and Wales. The 'steam tour' features most prominently, since the more spectacular pictures are always to be obtained when steam locomotives are hauling heavily-laden trains (especially along steeply graded lines), but an additional attraction of the book is the number of 'Hush-hush' trips that have taken place of recent years, often over routes not normally open to steam, but which the authors have succeeded in discovering and photographing. Some slight coverage is also given to 'On Shed' shots, but only where associated Rail Tours are concerned, or when the particular locomotive has impending main-line movement. Most depots with active main-line locos are shown.

It was on 11 August 1968 that steam officially finished on British Railways — except for the narrow-gauge branch line to Devil's Bridge, and *Flying Scotsman* which, under a previous agreement, could still be used for a few more years to haul specials. But for the many hundreds of still-serviceable standard-gauge steam locomotives, it was all over. Not that steam ended with a whisper; it went in a glorious spectacle of defiance, for who will ever forget the performance of the Bullied Pacifics on the Waterloo-Bournemouth line in the summer of 1967, for example, or the final fling of the Black Fives in the Preston area during the first half of 1968?

To the many thousands of enthusiasts who pilgrimaged to the last remaining pockets of steam at that time, it was very sad, and all the more so because it was happening so quickly. It really was a case of here today and gone tomorrow, and if ever the expression 'Now you see it, now you don't' had any significance, surely this was it. Whilst, area by area, steam was disappearing, the realisation gradually sank in that never again were to be seen the

idols of one's youth, pounding away up Shap or Lickey as they seemed always to have done. They were soon to be turned into motor cars and washing-machines after the ignominy of destruction in one or other of the many scrap-yards which were hurriedly being pressed into use for this very purpose.

What had come was . . . the end! British Rail had decreed that once steam had finished, it had indeed finished, and the operation of steam locomotives on its metals was totally prohibited, apart from the two exceptions already mentioned. Enthusiasts called this 'The Ban', and the level of interest in the national railway system seemed suddenly to drop away with only diesels to see. This was understandable. 'Boxes' they were called, as indeed they still are, devoid of beauty or romance, emitting foul-smelling odours and sounding like anything from a juggernaut to a jumbo jet. Nevertheless, however horrid diesels may be, photographing them demands utilisation of the scene as a whole, and, in a way, experience in that field has proved useful in obtaining many of the shots in this book.

In these circumstances, therefore, it was not surprising that the preserved railways really started coming into their own, especially since those already in existence (like the Bluebell and the Dart Valley Railways), were actually able to convey passengers through pleasant countryside behind historic steam locomotives over lines that British Rail no longer required, and were operated by teams of totally dedicated volunteers.

When eventually Mr Alan Pegler took his *Flying Scotsman* off to America in 1969, the only steam-operated service in British Rail's care was the 1 foot $11\frac{1}{2}$ inch gauge line out of Aberystwyth; but this was a tourist line in every sense, with trains running only in the summer months, to the waterfalls 680 feet up at the well known beauty-spot of Devil's Bridge. With well co-ordinated publicity, and assistance from its own Supporters Association, The Vale of Rheidol Railway has become one of the leading lights in the 'Great Little Trains of Wales' movement, and their three 2-6-2 Tank locomotives work all the trains between them, offering the visitor some of the most spectacular steam working to be seen in the British Isles.

In July 1969, British Rail relented slightly by holding an Open Day at Cricklewood Depot, and those who were fortunate enough to attend were offered the spectacle of three large locomotives, Class Five No. 5428, Jubilee No. 5593 *Kolhapur* and *Clun Castle*, hauling visitors up and down a specially selected stretch of track. During the day, the locomotives alternated, but there was always one on each end of the train, whilst the third stood back simmering in a siding. It was almost as if British Rail were trying to make up to the steam-lover for depriving him of his steam by offering him something rather special, but as it all took place in such a restricted area, it was, in effect, just a depot display, and afterwards, the locomotives returned to their museum home at Tyseley, such exhibitions being rarely repeated.

As a matter of fact, the nation actually owns some of the most historic locomotives still extant (the Bullied Pacific *Sir Winston Churchill* being one notable example), and occasionally British Rail has pulled them out of their hidey-holes to show them off at such places as Brighton. Although they have not been steamed (being simply static exhibits), they have aroused a lot of interest just by being shown.

It was to this state of affairs that Mr (later Sir) Richard Marsh came when he took over as head of the railways in 1971, and, being a real steam fan, an early duty was to arrange the very first 'Return to Steam' tour during October of that year. The idea was to discover if such tours were feasible, and if so, would they be popular? The loco chosen was *King George V,* with a train consisting of the five Bulmers Pullman coaches plus three standard bogies, and the route was to take in such towns as Newport, Birmingham, Swindon and London which, with stop-overs for exhibitions, would take eight days. The result was success beyond the wildest dreams of the organisers, the crowds flocking to see the train both at the lineside as it passed, and at the stations and sidings where it stopped, proving beyond any doubt that what the steam-starved rail-fan wanted was steam, and heralding the successful tours that were to come in the following years.

The capturing on film of so many of these tours has not been without its frustrations and disappointments. Unlike in the days of steam (pre-1968), if for any reason a locomotive should be missed, there would definitely not be another one along in a minute. Far from it, in fact, and consequently it is vital to the dedicated railway photographer that each opportunity is grabbed with both hands (and both cameras!), while it is still there to be grabbed.

The problem, however, is that the photographer of steam today is in a most unfortunate 'take it or leave it' position. Should the sun not be shining, or should the rain be pelting down, one just has to 'take it', and more often than not, it seems, the sun does *not* shine, and it *is* pelting down with rain.

And then there is always the unexpected. Steam locomotives have, on occasions, been known to fail, causing diesels to be substituted in their place at the last moment, to the consternation of all concerned. Fortunately this is not very common, it being far more likely that a camera will jam, or run out of film, that a tripod leg will get kicked, or that a carefully chosen and isolated viewpoint will, with the train in sight, suddenly become filled with the unthinking occupants of high-speed motor cars, ruining everything.

To overcome these and many other adversities requires an above-average degree of luck, and the authors readily acknowledge their good fortune over the years by offering this selection of photographs to all who love the steam locomotive (even in its preserved and highly polished state), and hope that their enjoyment in seeing them will at least approach our enjoyment in taking them.

David Eatwell and John H Cooper-Smith
1977

2 On Good Friday, 8 April 1977, the Vale of Rheidol's oldest locomotive, 2-6-2T No. 9 *Prince Of Wales* of 1902, nears Devil's Bridge with one of its first public trains (the 13.30 hrs from Aberystwyth) after being overhauled at Swindon during the 'closed' season. (DE)

1
Early Days

The end of the world had come for steam railway enthusiasts when British Rail not only finished with steam in (standard gauge) revenue earning service, but also enforced what was seen as a bloody-minded ban on all future excursions by preserved locomotives.

So came the doldrums, for between 1969 and 1971, no wheel turned on Britain's main railway system by the power of steam. But changes in senior railway management at this time brought a change in policy with regard to the preservation movement, and it was decided to experiment with the possibility of selling steam-hauled rail travel. Anticipated problems with watering, coaling and turning did not materialise, and provided the route to be used was well thought out, it appeared that there was still a

chance for steam to flourish on BR. Various routes became 'authorised', dependent mainly upon the availability of motive power, but these have never been exclusive, and although most steam-hauled tours take place on the lines between such places as Newport and Chester, and Tyseley and Didcot, circumstances have dictated alternatives (like the Marlow branch in July 1973), all of which gives variety to the steam preservation scene.

Things started quietly at first, locos going out one day and returning the next, but soon the various centres became adept at the quick turn-around, and from then on there has been no holding them. Steam was back again, and with a vengeance!

3, 4 On 12 July 1969, Cricklewood held an Open Day, the main attraction being three large 4-6-0 passenger locomotives, and in these pictures, the two ex-LMS types (No. 5593 *Kolhapur* and No. 5428, soon after receiving the name *Eric Treacy*) are shown on either end of a rake of coaches giving rides to visitors during the afternoon. Also present was *Clun Castle* which, in later years, was to work many rail tours, including the very first to carry members of the public on 10 June 1972. (DE)

5 Tyseley held an Open Day in 1969, similar to that at Cricklewood, and although this depot is privately owned, BR did allow a train to operate onto its rails.

Class Five 4-6-0 No. 5428 *Eric Treacy* ventures a short distance into 'foreign territory' with a four-coach shuttle, *Kolhapur* on the other end. (JHCS)

6 What might have been the last steam train on BR was run in the late summer of 1969 when, under Alan Pegler's ownership, the immortal *Flying Scotsman* made its last run, from Kings Cross to East Anglia, before shipment to the USA. (JHCS)

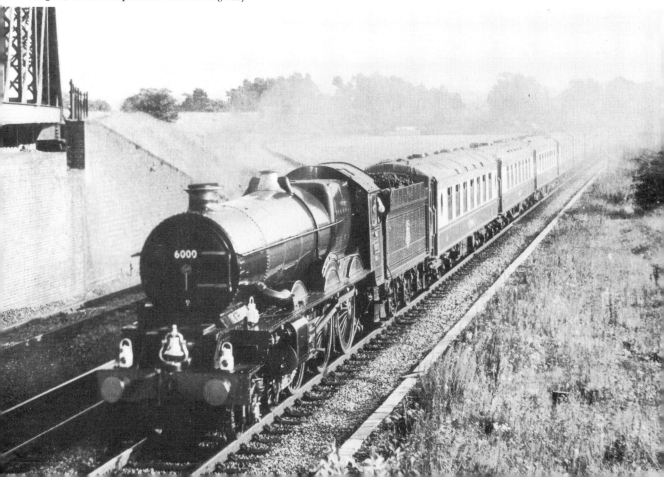

7-8 The tour that started it all. *King George V* nears Heyford (8) *above* and passes Aynho Junction (7) *left* on its way from Hereford and Newport to Birmingham with Bulmers Cider Pullmans and three extra coaches on the first afternoon of its 'Meet the People' eight-day exploration on Saturday 2 October 1971. (JHCS) (DE)

9 Two days later, No. 6000 returned from Birmingham to London (Kensington Olympia) with the Bulmers Pullman, leaving Saunderton Tunnel south of Princes Risborough shortly before lunch. (JHCS)

10 Steam had not been seen at High Wycombe for some years when *King George V* stopped for water (supplied by the local fire brigade) on Monday 4 October 1971, during the train's Birmingham-Kensington leg. Lunch-hour crowds flocked to the station, and were rewarded by this lengthy view of the pride of the GWR. (DE)

11 The whole procession returned towards home on the Thursday, heading westwards through Goring Gap on the way to Swindon. By Saturday it had reached Hereford, after one of the most triumphant 'Royal Tours' ever undertaken. (JHCS)

12 The first public steam-hauled rail tour since *Flying Scotsman* went to America was on Saturday 10 June 1972, when *Clun Castle* ran from Tyseley to Didcot in typical steam-tour weather . . . pouring rain! Here the train passes Claydon in the mid-morning murk. It returned next day. (DE)

13, 14, 15 On Saturday 17 June 1972, the first run of an A4 Pacific, in the shape of No. 4498 *Sir Nigel Gresley*, was made between Newcastle and Carlisle. The train nears Bardon Mill (13) on the outward journey, passing Brampton (14) on the return, and (15) accelerating away from Haltwhistle. (JHCS)

16 1972 saw the appearance of another A4 Pacific, No. 19 *Bittern*, which ran from York to Scarborough on 16 September, and is seen here negotiating the reverse curves near Malton. (JHCS)

17 Tyseley held an Open Day to welcome *Burton Agnes Hall* with a tour from Didcot on Sunday 1 October 1972, and a short length of BR track was allocated to *Princess Elizabeth* for giving rides to the public. The loco was on a brief visit from Ashchurch, and the train had another locomotive on the other end. It was Class Five No. 5428 *Eric Treacy*, shortly to leave for the North Yorkshire Moors Railway. (DE)

18 *Burton Agnes Hall* was painstakingly restored at Didcot after withdrawal from BR and its first main line tour was from its home depot to Tyseley and back on Sunday 1 October 1972. In this view the train is crossing the Leamington Road at Warwick on the return in the late afternoon, with two Great Western vintage coaches (also restored at Didcot) immediately behind the tender. (DE)

19 Jubilee Class 4-6-0 *Bahamas* has rarely been seen on rail tours, but one memorable occasion was on Saturday 14 October 1972, when the locomotive returned its train from Hereford (here departing at 15.40 hrs) to Shrewsbury, after *King George V* had brought it up from Newport. (DE)

20 GWR pannier tanks (0-6-0) were amongst the most numerous ever to have been built in this country, and quite a few have been preserved, but only one is known to have worked 'Return to Steam' rail tours and that was on Sunday 13 May 1973 (yes, it rained most of the time!) when No. 7752 ran back and forth between Birmingham (Moor Street) and Stratford-on-Avon all afternoon with seven well-filled coaches. This photograph is of the first train passing Earlswood Lakes on the return to Birmingham at about 14.00 hrs. (DE)

21 One of the many joys of railway photography is the unexpected, and on Sunday 10 June 1973, the 0-6-0 pannier tank was booked to repeat its performance of a month earlier, but shortly before the event it was 'failed' through what is believed to be vacuum problems. Consequently a substitute was required, and at short notice, *Green Arrow* took over on one of its first public appearances, thereby allowing the six coaches of the first train to be increased to ten for this, the second, here passing the golf course near Earlswood on the way to Stratford at about 14.45 hrs. (DE)

22 Scotland has not really had much steam, but on Saturday 30 June 1973, *Union Of South Africa* hauled six coaches from Inverkeithing to Dundee and back, and in the evening returned along the Firth of Forth, taking it very easy near Kinghorn. (DE)

23 On Sunday 15 July 1973, the centenary of the opening of the Marlow branch was celebrated by a 'Steam Day', and among many attractions was a shuttle service between Maidenhead and Bourne End, seen here near Cookham with 2-6-2T No. 6106 at the head of a six-coach train, and the smoke from *Burton Agnes Hall* just visible at the rear. (DE)

2
Away from Home

Many of the routes on which steam has been able to operate have a collection of preserved locomotives at one or other end, as, for example, Carnforth and Hereford. Sometimes locos from other collections have worked into these places, and in this section we see some of these 'foreigners' away from their home depots being serviced between trips, or stopping en route between steam centres. The most notable event which led to engines being seen far from their usual habitats was the Shildon Cavalcade in 1975. Some of the more unusual visitors to British Rail for this event are included in the following pages.

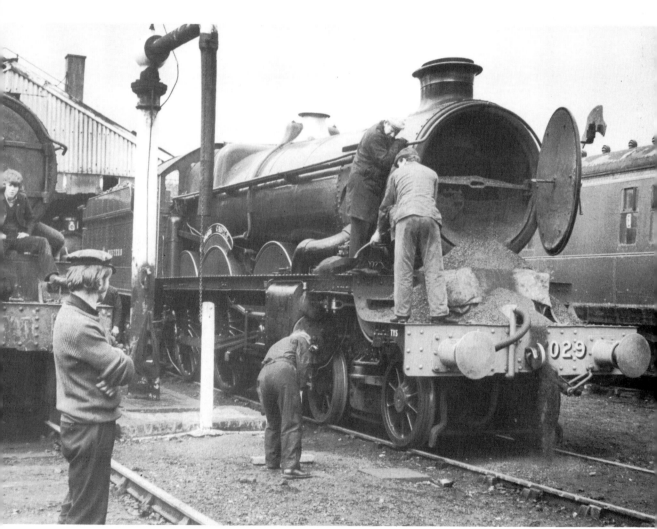

24 A slight case of clogging up! On arrival at Didcot, *Clun Castle,* having just hauled the first public steam-hauled train to run on BR for some years, is serviced in the early afternoon of Saturday 10 June 1972 in good time for the return to Tyseley next day. On the left, awaiting restoration, is sister loco No. 5051, *Earl Bathurst.* (DE)

25 After a very wet morning, the sun came out to shine on this fine array of power, lined up for the benefit of photographers outside Didcot shed at about 14.30 hrs. Left to right, the locomotives are: *Blue Peter, Pendennis Castle, Earl Bathurst* (awaiting restoration) and *Clun Castle* in steam, having worked down from Tyseley earlier in the day (10 June 1972), and still sporting the unique headboard 'Celebration Steam Run'. Just visible behind 7029 is 2-6-2T No. 6106, in the shed. (DE)

26 Gateshead MPD, about 08.00 hrs, 17 June 1972, and *Sir Nigel Gresley*, temporarily parted from its County Durham coal-mine home, darkens the surrounding sky after having its fire made up in preparation for the round trip to Carlisle (Steam Safari) later in the day. (DE)

27 A bit of spit and polish is applied to *Bahamas* at Bulmers Cider Depot, Hereford, during the afternoon of Saturday 14 October 1972, in readiness to return a train to Shrewsbury, once *King George V* had brought it back from Newport. (DE)

28 The sad story of 4472's sojourn in the USA, and its subsequent acquisition by Mr William McAlpine is too well known to be repeated here, but it was a great day in February 1973 when it finally returned home, and at about 17.00 hrs on Sunday 17, it sat on the site of the old steam shed at Edgehill (Liverpool) waiting to travel to Derby next day for a complete overhaul. Kneeling on the running plate is Mr Les Richards, the loco's 'keeper', and without whom it has hardly moved since. (DE)

29, 30 21 April 1973 was Easter Saturday, and on this date York held a 'Festival of Steam', involving two A4 Pacifics on BR, and various locomotives on the NYMRly. The 4-6-2s met at Scarborough, and since no turntable was available, they had to turn on the nearest triangle, which was at Filey Holiday Camp; *Bittern* carried out this manoeuvre round about 15.30 hrs (29). After the departure of No. 19 for Hull, *Sir Nigel Gresley* was left to its own devices (and most of the time in the rain!) in a bay platform at Scarborough while those passengers who had ventured further afield returned from Grosmont by bus to be steam-hauled back to York (30). (DE)

31 At about 07.30 hrs, and after much searching, *Union Of South Africa* was eventually run to earth sticking out of this shed at Kirkcaldy on Saturday 30 June 1973. Steam had already been raised prior to working one of the first 'Return to Steam' trips in Scotland, this one being a return journey between Inverkeithing and Dundee. (DE)

32 A unique excursion took place on Saturday 29 September 1973, when *Burton Agnes Hall* took a nine-coach train from Didcot via Banbury and Hatton to Stratford-on-Avon, and then on to Long Marston army camp. The locomotive turned on the Hatton triangle, and re-entered the depot (where it shunted the two vintage coaches for marshalling at the front of the train again) during a very heavy shower in the afternoon. (DE)

33 Large crowds (and a big 'box'!) watch Merchant Navy Pacific No. 35028 *Clan Line* detach itself from a special from Basingstoke at Westbury, preparatory to turning and servicing on 24 April 1974. (JHCS)

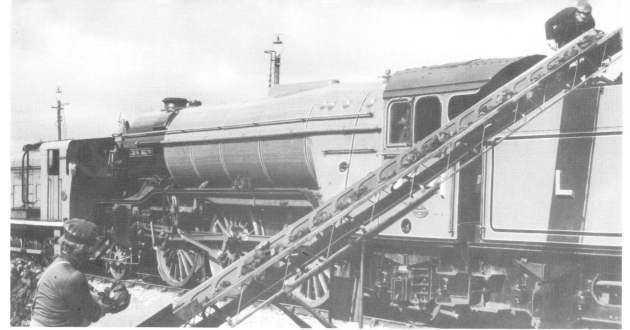

34 V2 2-6-2 No. 4771 *Green Arrow* being coaled at Carnforth on 15 June 1974, in readiness for working a return special the following day. (JHCS)

35 Anxious moments at Stratford as a suspect axlebox is looked at by the crew of *Clan Line* after arrival from Didcot on 26 October 1974. (JHCS)

36 *Union Of South Africa* makes an unscheduled stop at Haymarket shed after working a round trip to Dundee. On this occasion (7 June 1975) it ran short of water on the approach to Edinburgh, and was replaced by a Deltic for the last two miles into Waverley station. (JHCS)

37 The 'Rail 150' celebrations brought considerable variety of steam to BR. Here J27 No. 2392 (old NER No.) works the shuttle service between Shildon works and the station in typically inclement weather on Saturday 30 August 1975. (JHCS)

38 The sun shone gloriously for the Grand Cavalcade at Shildon, and all lined up, ready to go on Sunday 31 August are, from left to right, GWR 0-6-0PT No. 7752, LNER D49/1 4-4-0 No. 246 *Morayshire*, CR 0-4-4T No. 419, LNER 2-6-0 K1 No. 2005, NER 0-6-0 J27 No. 2392, NER Q6 0-8-0 No. 2238 and LMS Class 5 4-6-0 No. 4767 *George Stephenson*. (JHCS)

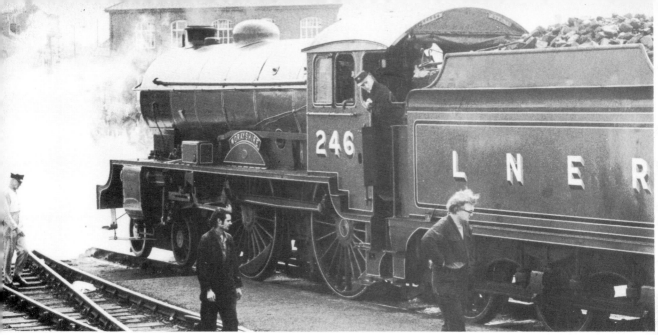

39 *Morayshire* shunts at Shildon, 31 August 1975. (JHCS)

40 *Sir Nigel Gresley* arrives at Newcastle Central on 7 September 1975, ready to work a 'Rail 150' special back to York. (JHCS)

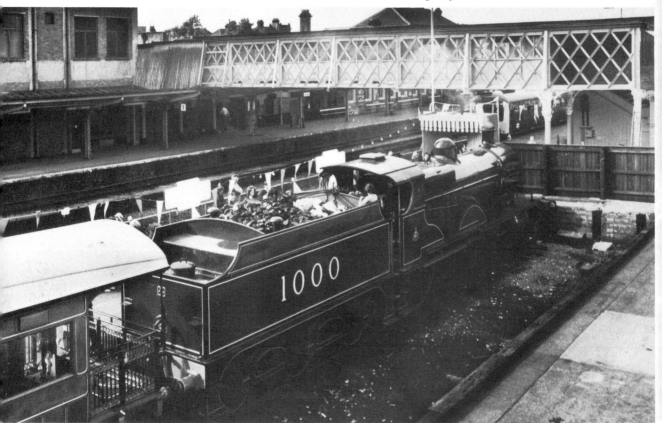

41 Whilst *Mayflower* and *Flying Scotsman* were double-heading a 'Rail 150' special down the East Coast Main Line on Sunday 21 September 1975, the Midland Compound No. 1000 was sitting in a sort of siding at Harrogate with a shirt-advertising train behind it, pretending to be in steam (a few old rags and some wooden crates were being burned in the firebox to produce the smoke coming out of the chimney!), and suffering the indignity of having people climbing all over it all day. Shame! (DE)

42 *Mayflower* and *Flying Scotsman* are serviced at Gateshead during the 'Rail 150' trip, ready to return their train from Newcastle to York. (JHCS)

43 LNWR Precedent No. 790 *Hardwicke* being turned at Carnforth to work specials with *Evening Star* to York on 19 June 1976. (JHCS)

3
Giants of Steam

To all who saw steam die in the 1960s, the saddest thing was that the biggest and most impressive locomotives were the earliest to be withdrawn. Here we see some of those which have been revived, not, unfortunately, on their former grounds of Beattock or Micheldever, but still on main lines. These largest of engines are not permitted over all routes, and are mainly concentrated on the line from Newport to Chester, but on occasion they do travel further afield, as some of these pictures show.

44 The original 'Return to Steam' special on 2 October 1971, *King George V* hauled, nears Heyford on its journey from Newport to Birmingham. (JHCS)

45 In typical Wiltshire scenery, *Clan Line* belts towards Salisbury near Warminster with the return Westbury-Basingstoke run of 27 April 1974. (JHCS)

46 *Clan Line* again, this time ascending Hatton bank on the Didcot-Stratford trip of 26 October 1974. (JHCS)

47 After an extended lunch, during which the loco turned and took water, *Clan Line* departs Stratford for the return to Didcot on the same day as the previous picture. To the great delight of sound recordists (like the gentleman holding the two microphones), the slipping of the loco as it got under way was considerable! Was it due to the size of lunch, one wonders? (JHCS)

48 On Sunday 20 April 1975, steam made one of its rare appearances on the Southern Region of BR when, in conjunction with an Open Day, David Shepherd's 9F 2-10-0 *Black Prince* ran between Westbury, Salisbury and Eastleigh. On the outward voyage, this powerful locomotive makes light work of hauling 14 heavily laden coaches near Wilton, shortly before the midday stop at Salisbury. (DE)

49 With the light almost faded away, and the sudden strong wind doing its best to blow the photographer out of the tree in which he was precariously balanced, *Black Prince* returns the 14-coach train from Eastleigh to Westbury, and with David Shepherd giving a friendly wave from his footplate, threads its way through Dean Woods at West Grimstead in the late afternoon. (DE)

50 Also on 20 April 1975, *Black Prince* nears Salisbury in the early evening (JHCS)

51 Being prepared for specials to Leeds and Sella-field, *Flying Scotsman* and *Green Arrow* stand over the ashpits at Carnforth on Saturday morning, 21 June 1975. (JHCS)

52 Leaving Newcastle by the King Edward Bridge, *Flying Scotsman* accelerates the curiously named 'Bristolian' southwards on Sunday 14 September 1975. This was one of the highly successful specials run over the East Coast Main Line in connection with the 'Rail 150' celebrations, commencing and terminating at Sheffield. (JHCS)

53 Earlier in the day, the much more aptly titled 'Tynesider' travelled northwards towards Newcastle, making a particularly spirited crossing of Plawsworth viaduct. (JHCS)

40

54 No. 4472 can usually be relied upon to give a thrilling display as it pulls away with a heavy load, and on Sunday 28 September 1975, there was no exception to this rule. *Sir Nigel Gresley* had brought the train from Sheffield (see picture **124**) to York during the morning, but on setting back onto it, *Flying Scotsman* experienced some difficulty in pulling off the brakes, and this was the result! Passengers on the train reported that this 'thrash' continued all the way to Newcastle, much to the consternation of officials, but delight of enthusiasts. (DE)

55 Crossing the High Level Bridge into Newcastle with the train shown in the last picture, is *Flying Scotsman*, obviously taking it easy after the exertions of the previous 80 miles, now that journey's end is in sight. (JHCS)

56 Spick and span, ready for a journey to Chester, *Clan Line* manoeuvres at Hereford on 23 April 1976. (JHCS)

57, 58, 59 *King George V* was booked to haul specials on Saturday 24 April 1976, but as the day approached, it became more and more obvious that it would not be ready in time, and a substitute would have to be used. But which loco? *Clan Line* was already booked for that date, so what was to be done? Almost at the eleventh hour, salvation came in the form of an offer from the Princess Elizabeth Society to use their loco, despite the fact that it was

widely advertised to make its debut run on 5 June. And so, the first public trips of the Stanier Pacific, No. 6201 *Princess Elizabeth,* took place completely unheralded — there just wasn't time — and most lineside viewers were expecting the *King* to put in an appearance. The great locomotive leaves Dinmore tunnel (57) northwards in the morning, and later in the day (58) (59) climbs Llanvihangel bank, north of Abergavenny. (JHCS)

60 To commemorate the epic run from Euston to Glasgow 40 years earlier, *Princess Elizabeth* ran from Hereford to Chester and back on 5 June 1976, showing the headboard used for the 1936 run, and displaying the Camden shed code (1B) which applied at that time. The train is heading north from Craven Arms. (JHCS)

61, 62 Saturday 23 April 1977 was a big day for steam lovers when two return trips ran from Hereford to Chester; motive power being the *King* and the *Princess* respectively. During the early hours of that morning the Pacific rests peacefully with banked fire outside Bulmers Cider Depot, whilst the 4-6-0, in similar state, enjoys the luxury and warmth of its own shed. Both locos were in readiness for the exertions which were to follow after daylight had broken (and the rain stopped!). (DE)

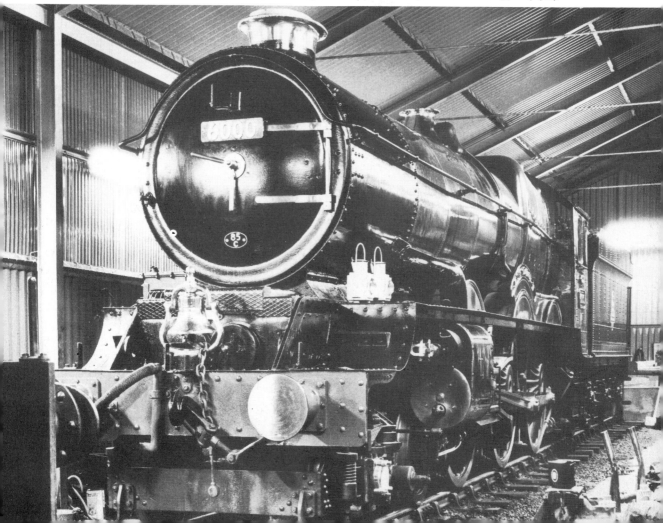

63 Right in his element, *King George V* lifts the Severn Valley Railway's GWR stock up Church Stretton bank en route for Chester on the morning of Saturday 23 April 1977, and later in the day . . . (JHCS)

64 All the majesty of the Stanier Pacifics is displayed as *Princess Elizabeth* blasts up Gresford bank with the same train of GWR coaches, returning to Hereford. (JHCS)

4
'Hush-hush'

Such is the popularity of steam today, that whenever it is announced that a steam-hauled train is to run on the main line, crowds of onlookers always flock to the route. They fill every vantage point, often for only a glimpse of the passing machinery, so that only the most inaccessable stretches of line are left un-occupied, and it is often quite a surprise to see how well some of one's photographs finally turn out.

However, steam locomotives occasionally move about the country without being generally advertised, and this opens up almost limitless possibilities to the photographer; not only because of the lack of competition for the best 'phot-spot', but also because these movements are often along 'rare' lines (as far as steam is concerned), and it is always an advantage to get an unimpeded view of the subject, especially when it is to be found in unfamiliar surroundings.

Not that all the pictures in this chapter are of 'non-steam' lines, but in each case there was no general publicity, and in most cases, the trip was very 'hush-hush' indeed.

65, 66 Since its return from the USA, *Flying Scotsman* had normally been housed in a shed at Market Overton (when it was not working in such places as the Torbay Steam Railway, for example), so it was a simple matter to run up the Midland Main Line, and then travel via Bedford (St. Johns) as it did on the morning of Saturday 30 March 1974, to get to Bletchley for an exhibition in connection with the passing of the old Bletchley borough. Despite a real 'pea-souper' earlier, the fog was starting to clear by about 08.00 hrs when the train stopped for a crew change on the St. Johns triangle, (65) and by the time it reached Lidlington some 50 minutes later (66), the mists had just about cleared sufficiently for this photograph to be taken at the north end of the station, with the brickworks chimneys just visible in the background. The train left Bletchley next day for Carnforth. (DE)

67 Locomotives sometimes start hauling their tour trains a long way away from where they are kept, and a case in point was on Saturday 6 April 1974, when these two, *Pendennis Castle* and *Flying Scotsman,* then resident at Hereford, started their respective trains to Shrewsbury from Newport. It meant a fairly early start, of course, and with the fog still hanging about in the Welsh hills, this unusual sight was to be seen at the northern approaches to Llanvihangel bank at about 08.00 hrs. (DE)

68, 69 *Pendennis Castle* was such a rare performer on BR that one would have expected its every move to be accompanied by batteries of photographers, but on Sunday 7 April 1974, this most definitely was not the case. The reason was that Mr William McAlpine had privately chartered a train from London in which his passengers travelled to Newport for the chance of riding behind steam to Shrewsbury, before returning to London. This private train was *Flying Scotsman* hauled to Hereford, and then 4079 took over for the second leg, nearing (68) and leaving (69) the level crossing north of Leominster. (DE)

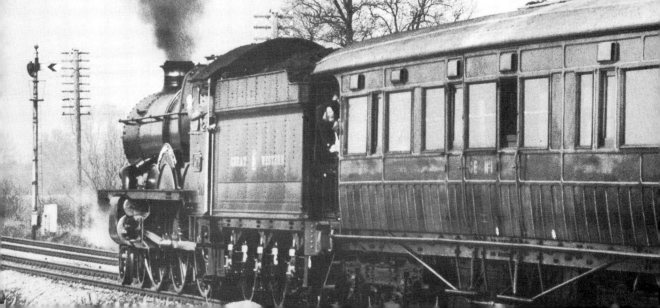

70 It was not actually a secret when *Green Arrow* hauled the first ever 'Return to Steam' excursion over the (now) popular route between Carnforth and Leeds, but the society which organised it found it fully subscribed from within the ranks of its members, thereby rendering any advertising an unnecessary luxury. The train nears Skipton eastbound on Easter Saturday (13 April) 1974. (DE)

71 This unusual view of the Forth Bridge was obtained from the South Queensferry side shortly before 09.00 hrs on Saturday 11 May 1974, just as *Union of South Africa* was running tender-first towards Edinburgh for a rail-tour, 'The Rid Lichtie', to Arbroath and back, later in the day. (DE)

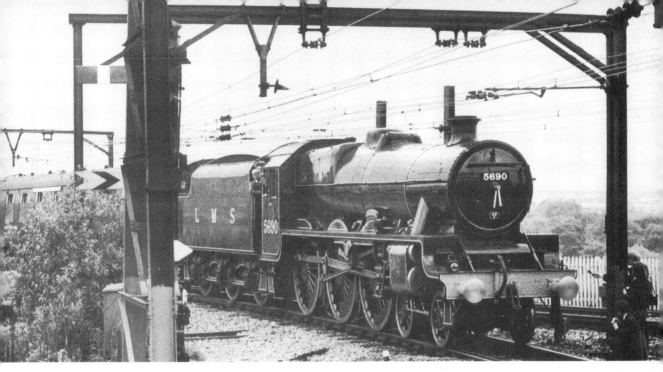

72 Steam under the wires. Not normally permitted, but an exception is this stretch of the Manchester (Piccadilly) to Sheffield (Victoria) line, where locos can work in and out of Dinting Steam Centre, as *Leander* is doing after taking an excursion to Sheffield (via Edale) from Guide Bridge on Sunday 16 June 1974. (DE)

73 When Clapham Transport Museum closed in 1974, a lot of the historic relics were dispersed, whilst most of the locomotives went into store prior to moving to York, and on Saturday 12 April 1975, this price-less trio took to the rails again for the journey north. Passing Millbrook (north of Ampthill tunnel) are *Mallard,* ex- LSWR Adams 4-4-0 No. 563 of 1893 (with the tender from the GER 2-4-0 NO. 490!) and the Stroudley Terrier *Boxhill* of 1880 riding on a well-wagon. (DE)

74 Pausing for water at Banbury at two o'clock in the morning of Monday 11 August 1975, during its trip from Didcot to Shildon, is *Cookham Manor* with some of the GWS vintage stock, and the footplate crew doing a bit of 'bull'. (DE)

75 After living at Ashchurch (near Tewkesbury) during most of its early life of preservation, *Princess Elizabeth* left there on 6 April 1976, for the move to Hereford. However, it was first necessary for it to visit Swindon Works for weighing, and early on the way there it rested briefly at Eckington before crossing over to the other line. At about 08.00 hrs, the crew took the opportunity to check the motion. (DE)

76 By about 13.15 hrs, the *Princess's* progress had reached the eastern end of Chipping Sodbury tunnel, and the longest of our preserved passenger locomotives is reduced to miniscule proportions in one of our deepest railway cuttings. (DE)

77 The journey up from Ashchurch included a water stop at Bristol (Parkway), and turning on the Stoke Gifford triangle; Swindon Works was reached by 14.00 hrs. (DE)

78 *Princess Elizabeth* crosses the River Wye at Chepstow at about 17.15 hrs, en route from Swindon to Hereford. Its stay on works was only three or four days, and on Saturday 10 April, it ran up to Didcot to turn on the triangle (at 74 feet 4 inches, or more, it was too long to fit on the Swindon turntable!). It then ran down to Bristol (water at Parkway again), up to Gloucester and down to Severn Tunnel Junction (for more water), and finally via Newport to its new home. The BSK (coach) with which it left Swindon developed a hot-box early on, and this parcels van, borrowed at Parkway, finished the journey, conveying members of the 6000 Locomotive Association back to Hereford. (DE)

79 During the winter of 1975/76, the opportunity was taken at Hereford to do some work on the motion of *Clan Line*, and in order to confirm that all was well, the loco did a round trip to Newport with frequent stops for oiling and examination. The weather was far from friendly, but this picture was obtained at Abergavenny at about 11.15 hrs, heading south. The work was obviously satisfactory, because only a few weeks later, 35028 kept good time at the head of the first of its many subsequent rail tours. (DE)

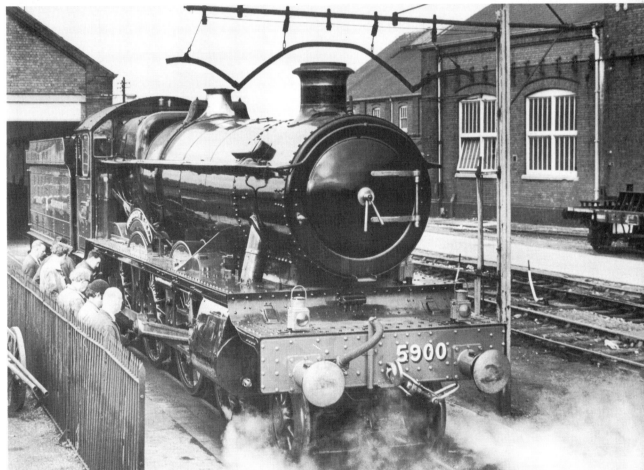

80, 81 Another locomotive which needed weighing before working a rail tour was *Hinderton Hall*, this one having been completely restored at Didcot during the preceding years, and on Monday 3 May 1976, it ran down to Swindon, was weighed (81 shows it setting back into the weighing shed under the critical eyes of some former GWR men!), and returned to Didcot, all in the space of a few hours. Two of the Great Western Society's vintage coaches accompanied the loco, and at about 07.30 hrs, the train passed the site of the old Wantage Road station (80). (DE)

82 It was a bitter blow indeed when the Midland Compound reached Carnforth on 24 April 1976, after double-heading an excursion from York with *Hardwicke,* and it was discovered that some of the boiler tubes were leaking. This meant that it would be unable to take charge of any of its rostered trains, including the Settle and Carlisle Centenary train on 1 May. As a result, it had to be returned to York Museum, and after a stay of exactly one month, it left Carnforth on 24 May, very gently hauled by *Flying Scotsman,* and passed near Bentham about 10.00 hrs. (DE)

83 One of the saddest events ever to occur in the field of steam locomotive preservation must surely have been when *Pendennis Castle* went off to Australia. After running to Tyseley from Carnforth on Friday 27 May 1977 and making a 'final fling' tour to Didcot and back on Sunday 29, it ran down to Avonmouth docks on Monday 30, travelling via Bromsgrove (down the Lickey) and Gloucester (where water was taken). At about 14.00 hrs it emerged from Wickwar tunnel, displaying the headlamp code of a parcels train! Why this was so was a mystery, because all the way to Gloucester, it had been an express; and quite rightly, since speeds in excess of 60 mph were easily reached on occasion. (DE)

84 *Pendennis Castle* is about to cross the M5 motorway as it nears Avonmouth docks, where it will be shipped to Australia a day or two later. (DE)

85 A farewell glimpse of *Pendennis Castle* in Avonmouth docks was obtained from across the fields soon after the locomotive arrived there about 15.00 hrs on Monday 30 May 1977. (DE)

5
Double-headers

To provide added interest to steam tours, it has often been the case that two locomotives have been used on a single train, and as a number of the centres where engines are kept have more than one example of similar power classes, it sometimes turns out that they can run in pairs; two Black Fives from Carnforth, for example, and various combinations of 4-6-0 from Didcot.

It has also been possible to run a number of very old smaller locos with the assistance of a larger and perhaps more reliable helper. Thus it has been on the 'Little North Western' to Carnforth that a LNWR Precedent 2-4-0 has once more been bouncing along, and the Midland Compound *should* have run more than the single occasion it did before major attention was required.

Longer trains can be used too, and some real mammoth ones have taken to the rails when pairs of large locomotives have been at the head, so that fifteen coaches on a steam-hauled train has not been at all uncommon, the increased revenue being more than welcome to the organisers.

86, 87 When steam started using the Barrow-in-Furness line out of Carnforth for 'Return to Steam' trips, there was nowhere available for locos to turn. This resulted in some strange sights along that route, like the day when two Class Five locos ran tender to tender, running round their train for the return trip so that the sight was similar. It was 4 May 1973 that Nos. 44871 and 45407 crossed Arnside viaduct on the return to Carnforth from Ravenglass (86). Picture 87 shows them in their home shed prior to the trip. (JHCS)

88, 89 As both *King George V* and *Flying Scotsman* had been to America (albeit 40 years apart!), it was decided to double-head them on a giant train between Newport and Shrewsbury, and so on Saturday 22 September 1973, no fewer than fifteen full coaches were to be seen at about 13.30 hrs being rushed up Llanvihangel bank in the rain. *Flying Scotsman* still sported its commemorative bell (88), and, with the locomotive positions having been reversed during the water stop at Hereford, neared Dinmore tunnel a couple of hours later (89). At Shrewsbury, 4472 went north with the Bulmers Cider Train on an exhibition tour, whilst No. 6000 returned the remaining ten coaches southwards, still wearing the 'Atlantic Venturers Express' headboard. (DE)

90 Saturday 19 October 1974 was the day they had all been waiting for at Didcot, for that was the first occasion their 'Vintage Train' ran: seven beautifully restored chocolate and cream GWR coaches, hauled by two equally beautifully restored locomotives, *Cookham Manor* and *Burton Agnes Hall*. At about 11.45 hrs this super sight passed Claydon (No. 7808 was also on its maiden outing since restoration), heading for Stratford-on-Avon (for lunch) and Tyseley, where the locos were serviced for the return direct to Didcot. Most of this journey took place in steady rain. (DE)

91 The second outing of the GWR Vintage Train was on Saturday 14 June 1975, when the combination ran over the little used (by steam) line via Worcester to Hereford. ZO8 heads west from Evesham, in the vicinity of (of all places) Upton Snodsbury and Wyre Piddle! (JHCS)

92 Since running in 1974, an additional coach had undergone restoration at Didcot, and was added to the 14 June 1975 run of the GWR Vintage Train to Hereford. Minus its distinctive headcode, it nears Worcester on the return trip in the afternoon. (JHCS)

93 Since steam returned to BR, the residents of Grange-over-Sands have had the opportunity to admire a wider variety of motive power than almost any other town in Britain, but on the evening of Saturday 21 June 1975, the only admirers of this sixteen-coach 'super-train', double-headed by *Mayflower* and *Green Arrow* back to Carnforth from Sellafield, were standing on the footbridge beside the photographer! (DE)

94 The same train as in the previous picture passes Silverdale, a few minutes after crossing the River Kent at Arnside, and nearing the home depot at Carnforth. To cover the same distance by road involves a lengthy detour round the river estuary, and about three times the length of time the train takes. So, even here, it *is* quicker by rail! (JHCS)

95, 96 Fifteen coaches on the East Coast Main Line. That was what *Mayflower* and *Flying Scotsman* hauled on 'The North Eastern' on Sunday 21 September 1975, as part of the 'Rail 150' festivities. Originating from Sheffield, this train was hauled by *Green Arrow* as far as York where it and No. 1306 should have carried on to Newcastle, but the V2 developed a hot-box on the tender, and was unable to continue, so 4472, at the shortest possible notice, stood in, and with minimal delay, saved the day! Travelling north (95), the train recovers from a signal check near Thirsk, and travelling south (96), the locos are taking it easy (despite the up-grade) near Aycliffe as the evening sun casts an almost horizontal shadow across the line (JHCS) (DE)

97, 98 What should have been one of the major events on BR in 1976 was the Centenary of the Settle and Carlisle Railway, but circumstances (and the weather!) conspired against the organisers, and things were not as had been originally planned. The Midland Compound and one of the Black Fives (both ex-LMS locos) had been booked for the festivities (1 May) and indeed this was to have been the highlight of No. 1000's visit to Carnforth from York. However, as the great day drew near, both had become unserviceable, so replacements were needed, and at very short notice indeed *Hardwicke* was used to pilot *Flying Scotsman* (which hurriedly returned from York where it was to have spent the summer) on the steam section to Hellifield. At about noon (97), the train of vintage and veteran stock passes near High Bentham, then, after sitting in a siding at Settle in the rain all afternoon, the two locomotives breast the top of the bank at Clapham (98) at the head of the return train in even worse weather. (DE) (JHCS)

99 *Hinderton Hall's* official debut, after being converted from a rusting hulk to the magnificent machine seen in this photograph by the 'magicians' at Didcot, was on Saturday 15 May 1976, when once again the Great Western Society's Vintage Train took to the track for a round trip to Tyseley, here passing Tackley in the morning. For the return, the locomotives changed places so that *Burton Agnes Hall* led. (DE)

100 Maximum use was very sensibly made of *Hardwicke* during its stay at Carnforth in 1976, and on 22 May it piloted *Flying Scotsman* as far as Ulverston where *Mayflower* took over the job on this heavy special to Sellafield, having run out light earlier. The tide was out (isn't it always?) at 13.15 hrs as the train is about to come off the Ulverston end of the Leven viaduct. (DE)

101, 102, 103, 104, 105 Five locos were in steam on Saturday 19 June 1976, for a series of specials between Carnforth, Leeds and York, and these photographs record something of the atmosphere of the day. On one of the eastbound journeys, *Mayflower* piloted Black Five No. 45407 near Long Preston (101) and Hellifield (102), and on another, *Hardwicke* and *Evening Star* slowed for signals near Bell Busk (103),

and (104) entered Bramhope tunnel. For the return trips, one train was (mainly) *Flying Scotsman*-hauled (not shown), and the second had the Black Five leading *Mayflower* back to Carnforth from Leeds. The headboard which on the outward trip had graced the front of *Hardwicke,* was transferred to this train (seen atop Giggleswick bank) (105), but was applied to the front of the second loco due to the fact that the lamp bracket on the smokebox door of the Black Five had been moved to the side in the days when it used to work under the wires. (DE) (JHCS) (DE) (JHCS) (DE)

106 Saturday 16 October saw similar events to those of 19 June, though somewhat less ambitious as only (!) three locos were used on this day. *Mayflower* and No. 45407 ran to Leeds, and *Evening Star* (with considerable light-loco movements) worked the stretch between there and York. The outward excursion, working hard, passes Gargrave at about 13.30 hrs. (DE)

6
Streamliners

The A4 class has more examples preserved than any other of the major Pacific types, and three of these have been allowed to haul excursions on British Railways. They are No. 4498 (ex-BR No. 60007) *Sir Nigel Gresley*, No. 19 (ex-BR No. 60019) *Bittern*, both restored to LNER Garter Blue, and No. 60009 *Union Of South Africa*, still in its BR green livery. They have represented streamlined Pacific power throughout Britain from South Wales to Aberdeen, and thanks to them, the mellow tone of their unmistakable chime whistles remains a thing of the present.

107, 108, 109, 110, 111, 112 Of the comings and goings on Easter Saturday 21 April 1973 (see pictures 29 and 30), these dramatic pictures can give a better account than mere words. *Sir Nigel Gresley* leaves York (in the rain) in the morning (107).

Bittern runs 'wrong-line' near Driffield on the way from Hull to Scarborough (108, 109), struggles with a

cross wind and an up-grade near Filey (110), heads
away from Bridlington (111), and makes for Driffield
and Hull (112) heading for home in the bright evening
sunlight. (JHCS)

113, 114, 115 'The Bon Accord' ran from Edinburgh to Aberdeen and back on 13 April 1974, using the 'Scottish' A4, *Union Of South Africa*. These shots caught it near the sea north of Stonehaven (113), southbound nearby (114) and in the late evening, on the climb to Lochmuir summit (115). (JHCS)

116 'The Rid Lichtie' (it was to be hoped that this name in no way reflected upon any of the facilities offered aboard!), ran from Edinburgh to Arbroath . . . mostly in the rain . . . but on the return in the evening, *Union Of South Africa* was bathed in glorious sunshine as it pounded up the incline at Ladybank, nearing Falkland Road at about 18.30 hrs. (DE)

117, 118, 119, 120 *Sir Nigel Gresley* made its first visit to Scotland since preservation on Saturday 22 June 1974, when it hauled an excursion between Edinburgh and Aberdeen. Leaving the Mound tunnel (117) in the morning, the train headed north over the Forth

Bridge and into the grey (118) out of Stonehaven in
the early afternoon. Having allowed passengers time
for a visit to the Granite City, 4498 returned over the
Tay Bridge (119) at about 18.30 hrs, and as the daylight turned to dusk, climbed to Lochmuir summit
(120), the day's exertions almost over. (JHCS) (JHCS) (DE)
(JHCS)

121 The trip to Dundee on 17 June 1975 had *Union Of South Africa* in charge, and since Edinburgh was as usual the starting point, another opportunity was taken to photograph a streamliner against the framework of the Mound tunnel. (JHCS)

122 The familiar background of York station is shown behind *Sir Nigel Gresley,* as it leaves for Newcastle on Sunday 7 September 1975, with one of the 'Rail 150' specials. (JHCS)

123, 124 Not originally booked for this tour, *Sir Nigel Gresley* was used instead of *Flying Scotsman* on Sunday 28 September 1975. *Sir Nigel Gresley* had failed a few weeks previously, and it was hoped that this might make things up to travelling enthusiasts. The train passed under the electrified GC line as it left Sheffield (123) and under the Great North Road near Burton Salmon (124) as it headed for York, where 4472 was waiting to take the 'Rail 150' special down the East Coast Main Line to Newcastle. (JHCS) (DE)

125 The Kirkcaldy Lions Club sponsored the 'Silver Jubilee Special' to Perth on Saturday 28 May 1977, which approached Gleneagles behind *Union Of South Africa* on the outward journey, being composed of both BR and preserved stock. (JHCS)

126 A good view of the corridor tender was obtained as *Union Of South Africa* slipped violently coming out of its shed at Markinch, ready to run light to Kirkcaldy for a special to Perth on Saturday 28 May 1977. (JHCS)

7
The National Collection

In 1975, the new central collection of preserved steam locomotives was assembled in the old steam shed at York, forming the major exhibits in the National Railway Museum. These engines are owned by the nation, rather than by private individuals, and are kept there with a view (so far as is possible) to occasional use by British Rail on steam specials. So far, *Hardwicke*, the Midland Compound No. 1000, *Evening Star* and *Green Arrow* have all done

this, whilst various ones of them (including the GNR 4-4-2 No. 990 *Henry Oakley*) have been loaned to preserved lines such as the Worth Valley Railway.

For the future, one may hope that the immortal *Mallard* and Stanier's masterpiece No. 46229 *Duchess Of Hamilton* will yet run again. However, considerable sums of money are needed to achieve this, not to mention time and expertise. We must wait and see.

127 *Green Arrow* roars out of Harbury tunnel on 1 July 1973, with a 14-coach Tyseley-Didcot special. (JHCS)

128 Both *Sir Nigel Gresley* and *Green Arrow* were used on tours on Saturday 6 October 1973; the former did two return trips between Newcastle and Carlisle, whilst the latter ran between Carnforth and Barrow-in-Furness. The first train out of Newcastle was 'The Hadrian' which, after arrival at Carlisle, ran up the main line (where its progress was temporarily halted on Shap by a stubborn cow!) for the second steam-hauled leg, caught here in full flight as it skirts the sea wall near Kent's Bank, at about 14.30 hrs. (DE)

129 GER 0-6-0T No. 87 of 1890, and the Midland Compound No. 1000, cross the River Ouse on the main line north of Bedford on their way from London (where they had been in store since the closure of Clapham Museum) to York. The coach in front of the 0-6-0T was absolutely bristling with policemen who mounted guard round the locomotives when they stopped just before this to have their bearings checked and greased. (DE)

130, 131 Since preservation, *Evening Star* has been seen most frequently on the line between York and Scarborough, but on the last day in May 1975, it hauled a special between Leeds and Carnforth, climbing towards Clapham summit (130) on the outward run, and, highlighted by the evening sun, returning (131) against the beautiful backdrop of Ingleborough. (JHCS)

132 Sunday 21 September 1975 was the day *Green Arrow* 'failed'. Brightside Station, near Sheffield, was the site of its passing towards York and Newcastle with a 'Rail 150' special on the last occasion one of these was to be double-headed. Unfortunately a hot-box developed on the tender of this loco, and the double-headed section between York and Newcastle featured *Flying Scotsman* (instead of 4771) with the B1 *Mayflower*. (JHCS)

133, 134 On Saturday 24 April 1976, two of our most venerable working locomotives, *Hardwicke,* with a maker's plate dated 1873, and the Midland Compound No. 1000 of 1902, exchanged places with *Flying Scotsman* by working a special train from York to Carnforth. The intention was that they should work from there all summer, but on arrival it was discovered that the Compound had boiler-tube trouble and could not be used. So, the only time this ancient combination saw service was on this occasion, near Gargrave (133) and at Arthington (134). (DE)

135 The only times *Hardwicke* has been entrusted
with its own train were on two Sundays in May 1976,
when it ran a shuttle between Carnforth and Grange-
over-Sands. Here it is shown crossing the Kent
viaduct at Arnside on 23 May, returning to base on
the last of its four trips that day. (DE)

136, 137 The oldest steam loco permitted to work the main lines is *Hardwicke,* and the youngest is *Evening Star.* These two were used on Saturday 19 June, 1976 to haul specials between Carnforth and York, passing near Clapham (136) about noon, and Bentham (137) a few minutes earlier. (JHCS)(DE)

138 A special was hastily organised using *Leander* between Guide Bridge and Sheffield, and *Evening Star* between York and Scarborough, to compensate for similar plans having been cancelled during the summer due to the water shortage and fire risk. Steam specials to Scarborough depend on the Filey triangle for the locos to turn, and since this facility has been threatened with withdrawal by British Rail, sights such as *Evening Star* thundering past Kirkham Abbey signal box on its way to the coast may exist only in photographs such as this, taken at about 14.00 hrs on Saturday 30 October 1976. (DE)

139 Eight locomotives hopefully await another tour of duty whilst on show in the National Railway Museum, York, on Friday 29 April 1977. From top left (clockwise), they are: GER Holden 2-4-0 No. 490 of 1891, NER Fletcher 2-4-0 No. 910 of 1875, Furness Railway 0-4-0 No. 3 (nicknamed *Coppernob!*), LNWR Webb 2-4-0 No. 790 *Hardwicke* of 1873, *Mallard, Evening Star*, (tender of) Midland Compound No. 1000 and rear half of the superbly finished (though unfortunately not working) Stanier Pacific No. 46229 *Duchess Of Hamilton.* (JHCS)

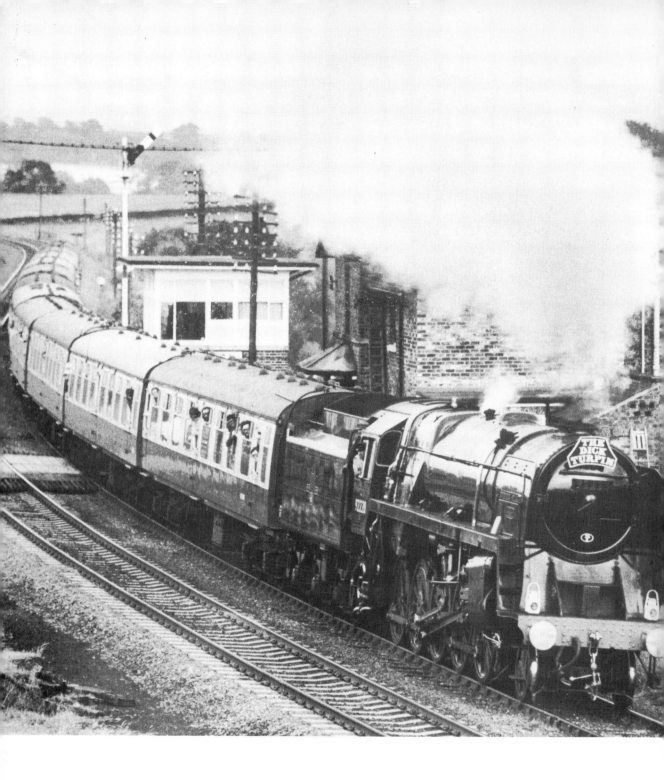

140 One of the longest one-hundred-per-cent steam journeys to be organised since 'The Ban' was that which ran, on Sunday 10 July 1977, the 263 miles between Carnforth and Scarborough. It used *Sir Nigel Gresley* to York, and *Evening Star* to the East Coast resort and back to Leeds. In the evening, the 9F sped its eleven-coach train westward past Barton Hill. (DE)

8
The 4-6-0

The ubiquitous 4-6-0 was latterly the commonest type of steam locomotive on British Rail and fittingly, many of these engines are preserved and permitted to work steam specials. In size, they range from the small Manor class of the GWR, up to the much more massive Castles and Kings. In between, and from some of the other railway companies, there is the all-purpose B1 class of the LNER, and from the LMS come the much-loved mixed-traffic Black Fives, and the express passenger Jubilees. The Halls (also GWR), are well represented too, and hopefully it may not be much longer before we see a Royal Scot in action once again as well.

141 An early duty for *Burton Agnes Hall* after restoration at Didcot was a special to Tyseley on Sunday 1 October 1972, and it travelled northwards at the head of its train (there being two of the GWS vintage coaches immediately behind the tender) across the rolling Oxfordshire countryside in the middle of the day. (DE)

142 After arrival on a special from Ravenglass on
5 May 1973, the Black Five eases onto the turntable
at Carnforth. (JHCS)

143, 144 The hills of Hathersage form a beautiful backcloth to *Bahamas*, working well with its ten-coach train from Guide Bridge to Sheffield on 17 June 1973 (143). Before the return trip, the loco sojourned

at Grindleford, having run up light from Sheffield, and is seen here (144) just nosing out of the three-mile long Totley tunnel on the way. (JHCS)

145 *Pendennis Castle* only hauled two public specials whilst in private ownership in this country, and the first of these was on Saturday 6 April 1974, when it worked a return between Newport and Shrewsbury. Soon after midday, it pounded northwards out of Caerleon, giving this rare sight of the fire through the open door. (DE)

146, 147 Most of *Leander's* outings since arriving at Dinting have been on the Hope Valley line, and Sunday 16 June 1974 saw no exception when shortly before 10.00 hrs, it was about to enter Cowburn tunnel (146) on the way from Guide Bridge to Sheffield, and a few hours later, coasted towards Chinley (147) on the return journey. (DE)(JHCS)

148 Deputising at short notice for a sister loco, and running late, Black Five No. 44932 slogs up to Clapham summit with a returning Leeds-Carnforth trip on 21 September 1974. (JHCS)

149 Due to the reluctance of BR to allow locos to push loaded passenger trains backwards, it is always necessary to have the loco on the front of the train it is moving, and so, when the Great Western Society's double-headed 'Vintage Train' arrived at Hereford on Saturday 14 June 1975, the leading loco *(Cookham Manor)* was detached in order that it could pull the train into Bulmers Cider Depot. No. 6998 *Burton Agnes Hall* is also being pulled, so this combination was a fairly slow mover, as can be imagined. (JHCS)

150 Although the B1 class was introduced by the LNER in 1942, No. 1306 was not actually delivered until early in 1948, by which time the LNER had ceased to exist, replaced by the nationalised BR. The works plate proclaims 1947 as the building date, but despite this, it was one of the first members of its class to carry its BR number (61306) from the time it appeared. The name *Mayflower* was added after preservation. On Saturday 21 June 1975, this beautiful green 4-6-0 sits under the ash plant at Carnforth, ready for the trip (double-heading with *Green Arrow*) to Sellafield later in the day. (JHCS)

151 'The Shakespeare Don' was *Clun Castle*-hauled between Birmingham, Stratford and Didcot on Saturday 17 April 1976, and, being sponsored by a local radio station, was full to overflowing with eager families (and some enthusiasts!), as it rushed through the beautifully maintained Wilmcote station in the early afternoon sunshine. (JHCS)

152 Black Fives proliferate in their preserved state, there being no fewer than a dozen examples spread about the British Isles, but it is always an event when one takes to the main line for the first time, and on Sunday 4 July 1976 this happened to the NYMR loco No. 4767 *George Stephenson*. The route chosen for the run was between Newcastle and Stockton (the train then went to York for a ride to Scarborough behind *Evening Star*) and at about 09.40 hrs passed Boldon Colliery on the outward section. (DE)

153, 154 Only one route in East Anglia is open for steam, and only one locomotive has been available to work it, so steam lovers in this part of the country can, with some justification, feel somewhat neglected. The line used is that from Manningtree to March (via Ipswich and Ely), and the loco is one that was saved from the Barry scrapyard, ex-SR S15 class 4-6-0 No. 841. On Saturday 18 September 1976, it was used to head a train over the permitted portion, passing Elmswell (153) at about 09.30 hrs, and nearly an hour later leaving Bury St Edmunds (154) on the way to March. (DE)

155, 156, 157 It was hard to imagine on Sunday 14 February 1970 that this vandalised and rusting hulk, languishing in the South Wales scrapyard at Barry, would (or even could) ever be returned to its former glory; but, it seems, all things are possible, and only a few years later, *Leander* was back in service, glowing gloriously in its new crimson-lake livery, and hauling loads as heavy as it ever had before, such as this Guide Bridge — Sheffield Special, photographed storming the bank out of Chinley (156) on Saturday 30 October 1976. The train continued to Scarborough (*Evening Star*-hauled from and back to York), returning from Sheffield at about 18.30 hrs in the dark (157), a magnificent sight indeed, but virtually unphotographable once it had departed. (DE)

158 *Clun Castle* worked two trains from the Birmingham area to Leamington and back on Sunday 3 April 1977, and soon after 05.00 hrs was being prepared in its shed at the Birmingham Railway Museum by the staff. (DE)

159 The second trip of the day took place in bright sunshine and No. 7029 was in fine fettle as it thrashed northwards up Hatton bank, making really sweet music. (JHCS)

160, 161 Having done a 'running-in' turn to Leeds from Hull a couple of weeks earlier, Class Five No. 5305 was all ready on Saturday 30 April 1977 to work the special between Leeds and York, which was to be its public debut. On the outward journey, Mr Draper's loco crossed the River Aire in the morning 'dim', but in the bright sunshine of the early evening it made a pretty picture leaving York (161), even though the regulator was closed, there being an adverse signal not far ahead. (JHCS) (DE)

162, 163 *Pendennis Castle* spent most of its active preserved life at Carnforth, unable to work trains out of the depot due to restrictions on its size, and it was eventually sold to Australia, to the great sadness of all British enthusiasts. To celebrate its passing, a special trip was arranged at very short notice, and the loco arrived at Tyseley a day or two before it set out with this farewell appearance on a train to Didcot. At about 12.30 hrs, it made this unforgettable attack on Saltley bank (162), whilst about an hour later it burst out of Harbury tunnel (163), making this magnificent and somewhat emotional spectacle. (DE) (JHCS)

164 The end . . . the end of this train, yes, but by no means the end of steam on British Rail, we hope. In these days of constant change (perhaps not always for the better), nothing is certain, but it is the fervent hope of the lover of steam that the authorities will not harden their attitude of tolerance towards the steam centres, and prevent them from putting their locomotives on BR metals. Here *Clun Castle,* at Aynho, is returning a train to Tyseley after a visit to Didcot on the evening of Saturday 17 April 1976. Even these signals have suddenly changed, for the previous October, they still sported their superb Great Western finials, and were still lit by oil, not electricity as now. But as 7029 disappears into the distance, we look forward to many more marvellous hours at the lineside, in the delightful company of our friends and colleagues, who enjoy and value with us the 'Return to Steam'. (DE)

Index

The numbers below refer to the numbers of the illustrations.